eave the field of battle."

*Shalok, Kabeer:*

*The battle-drum beats in the sky of the mind; aim is taken, and the wound is inflicted.*

*The spiritual warriors enter the field of battle; now is the time to fight! | |1| |*

*They alone are known as spiritual heroes, who fight in defense of religion.*

*They may be cut apart, piece by piece, but they never leave the field of battle. | |2| |2| |*

*- Bhagat Kabeer Ji - Sri Guru Granth Sahib Ji - Ang 1105*

This book is dedicated to the Shaheeds of the Khalsa Panth who fought to protect the weak, the homeless, the hungry and the oppressed.

# PREFACE

The role which history plays in shaping the character of future generations is often not given the prominence which it should deserve. In researching into the chapters of South Asian history, we at the Wahegru Foundation saw it as our responsibility to bring forth the depth of knowledge which is usually found in museums alone.

Undertaking the task at hand with much diligence and effort, our team began researching into the centuries old history of the Sikh, Mughal, Afghan, Persian, British and Hindustani influence on the Panjab.

In finding a treasure chest of history at our disposal, historical facts have been compiled into a digestible timeline spanning from the period of 1708 to 1843, in the hope that it would inspire both young and old to reflect on the heritage of previous generations. And in learning from the trials, tribulations and even the successes of the past, readers would be enabled to reconnect with and learn from such lessons of a bygone era.

# 1708 *to* 1762

## THE MUGHAL OCCUPATION

ਮੁਗਲਾਂ ਦਾ ਕਬਜ਼ਾ

# CONTENTS

## THE MUGHAL OCCUPATION

With the Indian subcontinent being persecuted by the oppressive regime of the ruling Mughals, and the invading Afghans and Persians, the people of Panjab suffer heavily during the turn of the 18th century.

It is during this time that the Khalsa Army stands as the protector of the common folk. As the Khalsa uses its hideouts in the jungles of Panjab to regroup and strategise, the tyrannical authorities of the time are left stumbling to hold on to the power which they had gained over so many centuries before.

As war ravages on, countless Sikhs pay the ultimate price by sacrificing their own lives for the protection of the weak, the homeless, the hungry and the oppressed. For each Sikh which attains Shaheedi in the field of battle, thousands more rally to support the cause of the Khalsa in bringing about freedom and self-determination for Panjab.

# Guruship Of Sri Guru Granth Sahib Ji

ਗੁਰਗੱਦੀ ਸ੍ਰੀ ਗੁਰੂ ਗ੍ਰੰਥ ਸਾਹਿਬ ਜੀ

1708: Sri Guru Gobind Singh Ji passes the throne of Guruship onto Sri Guru Granth Sahib Ji as the final Guru of the Sikhs at Nanded, later known as Takht Sri Hazur Sahib.

1708

੧੭੦੮

# Supreme Command Of Baba Banda Singh Ji Bahadur

ਮੁਖੀ ਬਾਬਾ ਬੰਦਾ ਸਿੰਘ ਜੀ
ਬਹਾਦਰ ਦੀ ਅਗਵਾਈ

1708: Sri Guru Gobind Singh Ji appoints Baba Banda Singh Ji Bahadur as the Mukhi, Supreme Commander, of the Khalsa Panth.

# Retirement Of Mata Bhag Kaur Ji from Active Service

ਮਾਤਾ ਭਾਗ ਕੌਰ ਜੀ ਨੇ ਆਪਣੀ ਜ਼ਿੰਦਗੀ ਦਾ ਅਖੀਰਲਾ ਸਮਾਂ ਭਜਨ ਬੰਦਗੀ ਵਿਚ ਬਿਤੀਤ ਕੀਤਾ

1708: Mata Bhag Kaur Ji (Mai Bhago), famous for leading the 40 Mukte (liberated ones) into battle in 1705, retires from active service and settles down in Jinvara, 11km from Bidar in Karnataka, India, where, immersed in meditation, she passes away at an old age.

# Passing Of Bhai Daya Singh Ji & Bhai Dharam Singh Ji

ਅਕਾਲ ਚਲਾਣਾ ਭਾਈ ਦਇਆ ਸਿੰਘ ਜੀ ਅਤੇ ਭਾਈ ਧਰਮ ਸਿੰਘ ਜੀ

1708: Bhai Daya Singh Ji and Bhai Dharam Singh Ji, the final two surviving Panj Pyare pass away in Nanded after retiring from active service. Bhai Mokham Singh Ji, Bhai Himmat Singh Ji and Bhai Sahib Singh Ji had attained Shaheedi earlier in 1705 in the Battle of Chamkaur alongside Sahibzada Ajit Singh Ji and Sahibzada Jujhar Singh Ji. Bibi Sharan Kaur Ji took on the seva of performing the last rites of the Shaheeds on the battlefield, for this she too attained Shaheedi upon being caught by the Mughals and thrown into the funeral pyre.

1710

੧੭੧੦

# Baba Banda Singh Ji Bahadur Enters Sirhind

ਬਾਬਾ ਬੰਦਾ ਸਿੰਘ ਜੀ ਬਹਾਦਰ ਦਾ ਸਰਹੰਦ ਵਿਚ ਦਾਖਲ ਹੋਣਾ

1710: Baba Banda Singh Ji Bahadur enters Sirhind and declares the first Khalsa Raaj. Bhai Fateh Singh Ji assassinates Wazir Khan to avenge the Shaheedi of Sahibzada Zorawar Singh Ji and Sahibzada Fateh Singh Ji.

1710

੧੭੧੦

# Cremation Of Bibi Anoop Kaur Ji

ਅੰਤਿਮ ਸੰਸਕਾਰ ਬੀਬੀ ਅਨੂਪ ਕੌਰ ਜੀ

1710: Baba Banda Singh Ji Bahadur and the Khalsa Army dig up Bibi Anoop Kaur Ji's buried remains at Malerkotla in order to cremate her according to the code of conduct of Khalsa Rehat. A few years earlier in 1705, after being separated from the Khalsa Army at the River Sirsa, Bibi Anoop Kaur Ji managed to regroup with 5 Sikhs in an attempt to rescue Mata Gujar Kaur Ji, Sahibzada Zorawar Singh Ji and Sahibzada Fateh Singh Ji from Sirhind. The 5 Sikhs attained Shaheedi after being intercepted by Mughal forces along the way, Bibi Anoop Kaur Ji's life was spared and she was held captive by the Mughals. After refusing to convert to Islam and refusing to marry the Mughal Governor, she attained Shaheedi by forcefully taking a dagger from a Mughal guard's sheath and thrusting it into her own chest.

1713

੧੭੧੩

# Passing Of Bhai Nand Lal Singh Ji

ਅਕਾਲ ਚਲਾਣਾ ਭਾਈ ਨੰਦ ਲਾਲ ਸਿੰਘ ਜੀ

1713: Bhai Nand Lal Singh Ji, one of Sri Guru Gobind Singh Ji's closest poets, passes away in Multan after spending the later few years of his life preaching Sikhi and establishing a school of Arabic and Persian.

# Shaheedi Of Baba Banda Singh Ji Bahadur & The Khalsa Warriors

੭੦੦ ਸਿੰਘਾਂ ਸਮੇਤ ਬਾਬਾ ਬੰਦਾ ਸਿੰਘ ਜੀ ਬਹਾਦਰ ਦੀ ਸ਼ਹੀਦੀ

1716: Baba Banda Singh Ji Bahadur, Bhai Fateh Singh Ji, Bhai Baj Singh Ji and 700 of the Khalsa warriors attain Shaheedi at Delhi. Baba Ajai Singh Ji, the young son of Baba Banda Singh Ji Bahadur, also attains Shaheedi after having his heart thrust out and force fed to his father.

1716

੧੭੧੬

# Shaheedi Of Bibi Shushil Kaur Ji

ਬੀਬੀ ਸੁਸ਼ੀਲ ਕੋਰ ਜੀ ਦੀ ਸ਼ਹੀਦੀ

1716: Bibi Shushil Kaur Ji, the wife of Baba Banda Singh Ji Bahadur attains Shaheedi after refusing to convert to Islam and refusing to marry her Mughal captor. In the same manner of Bibi Anoop Kaur Ji, Bibi Shushil Kaur Ji forcefully takes a dagger from a Mughal guard's sheath and thrusts it into her own chest.

# Hindu Families Support The Khalsa Army

ਨਿਰਮਲ ਪੰਥੀ ਸਿੱਖਾਂ ਦੇ ਪ੍ਰਚਾਰ ਸਦਕਾ, ਹਿੰਦੂ ਪਰਵਾਰਾਂ ਦਾ ਇੱਕ ਬੱਚਾ ਸਿੱਖ ਸਜ ਕੇ, ਖਾਲਸਾ ਫੌਜ ਵਿਚ ਭਰਤੀ ਹੋ ਕੇ, ਜ਼ੁਲਮ ਦੇ ਖਾਤਮੇ ਲਈ ਤਤਪਰ ਹੋ ਜਾਂਦਾ

1720's: As the 18th century begins to take a turn for ever more persecution by the ruling Mughals and the invading Afghans and Persians. Hindu families in Panjab begin raising their first born as Sikhs so as to enlist them into the Khalsa Army, to support the Khalsa's efforts of defending the poor and innocent people of India. This effort is supported by the Nirmale Sikhs in bringing new recruits into the Khalsa Army.

੧੭੨੧

# Appointment Of Bhai Mani Singh Ji As Head Granthi Of Sri Harmandir Sahib

ਭਾਈ ਮਨੀ ਸਿੰਘ ਜੀ ਸ੍ਰੀ ਹਰਿਮੰਦਰ ਸਾਹਿਬ ਦੇ ਹੈਡ ਗ੍ਰੰਥੀ ਮਥਾਪਤ ਕੀਤੇ ਗਏ

1721: Bhai Mani Singh Ji (the brother of Bhai Dayal Das Ji, who attained Shaheedi alongside Sri Guru Tegh Bahadur Ji) is appointed as Head Granthi at Sri Harmandir Sahib by Sri Guru Gobind Singh Ji's wife, Mata Sundar Kaur Ji. He brings about peace between the Tat Khalsa (the true Khalsa who believed in the Guruship of Sri Guru Granth Sahib Ji) and Bandai Khalsa (followers of Baba Banda Singh Ji Bahadur who began to regard Baba Banda Singh Ji Bahadur as their Guru). Bandai Khalsa sought control over Panthic matters but Tat Khalsa refused, stating there should not be any division in the Khalsa Panth

1721

੧੭੨੧

# Compilation Of Sri Dasam Granth Ji

## ਸ੍ਰੀ ਦਸਮ ਗ੍ਰੰਥ ਜੀ ਦਾ ਸੰਪਾਦਨ

1721: Under the command of Mata Sundar Kaur Ji, Bhai Mani Singh Ji and Bhai Shia Singh Ji begin collecting the writings of Sri Guru Gobind Singh Ji and compiling them into Sri Dasam Granth Ji.

# Gathering Of Sarbat Khalsa

## The Threefold Plan

ਸਰਬੱਤ ਖਾਲਸਾ : ਨਵੀਂ ਜੰਗੀ ਯੋਜਨਾ ਤਿਆਰ ਕੀਤੀ ਗਈ

1726: Sarbat Khalsa is held with the announcement of a threefold plan of action:

1.  To plunder government treasures in transit between local and regional offices and the central treasury;

2.  To raid government armouries for weapons and government stables for horses and carriages;

3.  To eliminate government informers and lackeys.

# Gathering Of Sarbat Khalsa:

## The Supreme Command Of Nawab Kapur Singh Ji

ਸਰਬੱਤ ਖ਼ਾਲਸਾ : ਨਵਾਬ ਕਪੂਰ ਸਿੰਘ ਜੀ ਨੂੰ ਅਕਾਲ ਤਖ਼ਤ ਦਾ ਮੁਖੀ ਸਥਾਪਤ ਕੀਤਾ ਗਿਆ

1733: Sarbat Khalsa is held. Bhai Subegh Singh Ji, a government contractor at the time, is sent as an envoy to negotiate a Peace Treaty on behalf of the Mughal Governor Zakharia Khan. Bhai Subegh Singh Ji is first made to seek forgiveness from the Khalsa for his loyalty to the Mughals. After the Khalsa accepts the terms of the Peace Treaty, Nawab Kapur Singh Ji (Singhpuria Misl) is chosen as Mukhi, Supreme Commander, of the Khalsa Panth. The Panj Pyare who appoint the Nawabi include: Baba Deep Singh Ji (Shaheeda Misl), Bhai Jassa Singh Ji (Ramgarhia Misl), Bhai Hari Singh Ji (Bhangi Misl), Bhai Budh Singh Ji (Maharaja Ranjit Singh Ji's great great grandfather) and Bhai Karam Singh Ji. The Khalsa Army is organised into Buddha Dal and Tarna Dal. Nawab Kapur Singh Ji (Singhpuria Misl), along with Bhai Sham Singh Ji, Baba Gurbakhsh Singh Ji, Bhai Bagh Singh Ji, Bhai Gurdial Singh Ji and Bhai Sukha Singh Ji lead the Buddha Dal regiments. Bhai Jassa Singh Ji (Ramgarhia Misl) and Bhai Jassa Singh Ji (Ahluwalia Misl) lead the Tarna Dal regiments under the command of Bhai Hari Singh Ji (Bhangi Misl).

# Passing Of Mata Sahib Kaur Ji

ਅਕਾਲ ਚਲਾਣਾ ਮਾਤਾ ਸਾਹਿਬ ਕੌਰ ਜੀ

1733: Mata Sahib Kaur Ji, the mother of the Khalsa passes away in Delhi. Gurdwara Bala Sahib now stands at this location in her memory.

# Shaheedi Of Bhai Mani Singh Ji & Family

ਭਾਈ ਮਨੀ ਸਿੰਘ ਜੀ ਅਤੇ ਉਹਨਾਂ ਦੇ ਪਰਿਵਾਰ ਦੀ ਸ਼ਹੀਦੀ

1737: Bhai Mani Singh Ji attains Shaheedi by being cut limb by limb for refusing to pay taxes to the Mughals. Members of his family are also rounded up and attain Shaheedi. Upon hearing this news, Nawab Kapur Singh Ji (Singhpuria Misl) takes personal command of a mission to assassinate Zakharia Khan at the Badshahi Mosque in Lahore. The mission is unsuccessful as Zakharia Khan does not show up. However, Bhai Ajmer Singh Ji (Bhai Mani Singh Ji's nephew) successfully kidnaps the Qazi who ordered the execution of Bhai Mani Singh Ji and the Qazi is assassinated by the Khalsa.

# Persian Invasion Of India

## ਭਾਰਤ ਉਤੇ ਇਰਾਨੀਆਂ ਦਾ ਹਮਲਾ

1738 - 1739: Persians invade India under the command of Nadir Shah to plunder and pillage the subcontinent.

# Shaheedi Of Bhai Bota Singh Ji & Bhai Garja Singh Ji

ਭਾਈ ਬੋਤਾ ਸਿੰਘ ਜੀ ਅਤੇ ਭਾਈ ਗਰਜਾ ਸਿੰਘ ਜੀ ਦੀ ਸ਼ਹੀਦੀ

1739: Upon hearing the common people of Panjab saying that the Mughal authorities had wiped out the Sikhs, Bhai Bota Singh Ji and Bhai Garja Singh Ji proclaim Khalsa Raaj at a busy trade route junction, charging wealthy traders a tax to travel into territory claimed by the Khalsa, in order to prove that the Sikhs are still alive and well. Bhai Bota Singh Ji and Bhai Garja Singh Ji both attain Shaheedi after battling with Mughal forces who are alerted of the incident.

# Mughal Invasion Of Sri Harmandir Sahib

ਸ੍ਰੀ ਹਰਿਮੰਦਰ ਸਾਹਿਬ ਉਤੇ ਮੁਗਲਾਂ ਦਾ ਕਬਜ਼ਾ

1740: Learning that the Sikhs drew their strength from the Sarovar at Sri Harmandir Sahib, Masa Ranghar invades Sri Harmandir Sahib and bans Sikhs from approaching the complex. In an act of defiance, the Sikhs begin organising raiding bands to either charge or sneak past Mughal guards to bathe in the Sarovar, shouting Jakarai of 'Jo Bole So Nihaal, Sat Sri Akal' as they raced back into their jungle hideouts. Bhai Mansha Singh Ji is one of the many who attains Shaheedi whilst bathing in the Sarovar.

# Khalsa Army Assassinates Masa Ranghar

ਖ਼ਾਲਸਾ ਫ਼ੌਜ ਵੱਲੋਂ ਮੱਸਾ ਰੰਘੜ ਦਾ ਮੌਤ

1740: After Masa Ranghar takes over and converts Sri Harmandir Sahib into his own court and brothel, Bhai Sukha Singh Ji and Bhai Mehtab Singh Ji are tasked with assassinating Masa Ranghar for the desecration of Sri Harmandir Sahib. Masa Ranghar's head is severed from his body and brought back to the Khalsa as a trophy.

# Shaheedi Of Bhai Subegh Singh Ji & Bhai Shabaz Singh Ji

ਭਾਈ ਸੁਬੇਗ ਸਿੰਘ ਜੀ ਅਤੇ ਭਾਈ ਸ਼ਾਹਬਾਜ਼ ਸਿੰਘ ਜੀ ਦੀ ਸ਼ਹੀਦੀ

1745: Bhai Subegh Singh Ji (the government contractor who acted as envoy for Zakharia Khan during the 1733 Peace Treaty with the Khalsa), and his son Bhai Shabaz Singh Ji, attain Shaheedi for refusing to convert to Islam and for refusing to be forcefully married into a Muslim family. Both Bhai Subegh Singh Ji and Bhai Shabaz Singh Ji are crushed on a spiked wheel for their defiance against the Mughals.

# Gathering Of Sarbat Khalsa:

## Reorganisation Of The Khalsa Army

ਸਰਬੱਤ ਖਾਲਸਾ: ੨੫ ਮਿਸਲਾਂ ਦੀ ਸਥਾਪਨਾ

1745: Sarbat Khalsa is held. The Khalsa Army is reorganised into 25 regiments by Nawab Kapur Singh Ji.

# Shaheedi Of Bhai Taru Singh Ji & Bhai Mehtab Singh Ji

ਭਾਈ ਤਾਰੂ ਸਿੰਘ ਜੀ ਅਤੇ ਭਾਈ ਮਹਿਤਾਬ ਸਿੰਘ ਜੀ ਦੀ ਸ਼ਹੀਦੀ

1745: Bhai Taru Singh Ji is arrested by Mughal authorities, his scalp is removed for refusing to cut his Kes and convert to Islam. Upon hearing of Bhai Taru Singh Ji's arrest, Bhai Mehtab Singh Ji (who assassinated Masa Ranghar in 1740), hands himself in to the Mughal authorities so as to ensure that Bhai Taru Singh Ji does not undergo his ordeal alone. Bhai Taru Singh Ji attains Shaheedi from the loss of blood from his scalp being removed, Bhai Mehtab Singh Ji attains Shaheedi by being crushed on a spiked wheel.

# Mughal Attack On Sri Harmandir Sahib

ਸ੍ਰੀ ਹਰਿਮੰਦਰ ਸਾਹਿਬ ਉਤੇ ਮੁਗਲਾਂ ਦਾ ਹਮਲਾ

1746: Lakhpat Rai, a Hindu Diwan of the Mughal court of Lahore attacks Sri Harmandir Sahib.

# Khalsa Army Assassinates Jaspat Rai

ਖ਼ਾਲਸਾ ਫੌਜ ਵੱਲੋਂ ਜਸਪਤ ਰਾਏ ਦਾ ਕੌਤਲ

1746: Bhai Nibahu Singh Ji beheads the Mughal commander Jaspat Rai, (also the brother of Lakhpat Rai) in the heat of battle by catching hold of the tail of Jaspat Rai's elephant, leaping on to its back, striking off Jaspat Rai's head with a single blow of his sword and then jumping down holding Jaspat Rai's head in his hands. The Mughal forces flee the battlefield in terror after seeing this.

# Chhota Ghalughara

## The Small Genocide

ਛੋਟਾ ਘੱਲੂਘਾਰਾ ਜਿਸ ਵਿਚ ਤਕਰੀਬਨ ੧੫,੦੦੦ ਸਿੱਖ ਸ਼ਹੀਦ ਹੋਏ

1746: Chhota Ghalughara, the Small Genocide. Around 10,000 to 15,000 Sikhs lose their lives and attain Shaheedi in the heat of survival against Mughal forces.

# First Afghan Invasion Of India

ਭਾਰਤ ਉਤੇ ਪਹਿਲਾ ਅਫਗਾਨੀ
ਹਮਲਾ

1747 - 1748: First Afghan Invasion of India under the command of Ahmad Shah Abdali to plunder and pillage the subcontinent. Bibi Ranjit Kaur Ji of the Khalsa Army is tasked with gathering intelligence on Ahmad Shah Abdali's troops.

# Passing Of Mata Sundar Kaur Ji

ਅਕਾਲ ਚਲਾਣਾ ਮਾਤਾ ਸੁੰਦਰ ਕੌਰ ਜੀ

1747: Mata Sundar Kaur Ji, the wife of Sri Guru Gobind Singh Ji passes away in Delhi. Gurdwara Bala Sahib now stands at this location in her memory.

# Mir Mannu's Jails

ਮੀਰ ਮੰਨੂ ਦੀ ਜੇਹਲ ਵਿਚ ਸ਼ਹੀਦੀਆਂ

1748: Mir Mannu becomes Governor of Lahore and begins his genocide of the Sikhs of Panjab. Every Sikh has a price placed upon their head and many Sikhs are executed within his jails. Women are captured and witness their young children being flung onto Mughal spears. Bibi Baghel Kaur Ji of the Khalsa Army successfully establishes a task force and begins rescuing women entrapped in Mir Mannu's jails. Bibi Bhagel Kaur Ji is eventually caught by the Mughals, tortured and attains Shaheedi.

# Gathering Of Sarbat Khalsa

## The Supreme Command Of Bhai Jassa Singh Ji

### *(Ahluwalia Misl)*

ਸਰਬੱਤ ਖਾਲਸਾ: ਭਾਈ ਜੱਸਾ ਸਿੰਘ ਜੀ
(ਆਹਲੂਵਾਲੀਆ ਮਿਸਲ) ਨੂੰ ਅਕਾਲ
ਤਖਤ ਦਾ ਮੁਖੀ ਸਭਾਪਤ ਕੀਤਾ ਗਿਆ

1748: Sarbat Khalsa is held. Nawab Kapur Singh Ji (Singhpuria Misl) hands over the seva of Mukhi, Supreme Command, of the Khalsa Panth to Bhai Jassa Singh Ji (Ahluwalia Misl). Bhai Jassa Singh Ji (Ahluwalia Misl) reorganises the Khalsa Army into 11 Misls.

# Construction Of Ramrauni Bunga

ਰਾਮਰੌਣੀ ਬੁੰਗੇ ਦੀ ਉਸਾਰੀ

1748: The fort of Ramrauni Bunga is built next to Sri Harmandir Sahib.

# Mughal Attack On Ramrauni Bunga

ਰਾਮਰੌਣੀ ਬੁੰਗੇ ਉਤੇ ਮੁਗਲਾਂ ਵੱਲੋਂ ਹਮਲਾ

1748: Under the orders of Mir Mannu, the fort of Ramrauni Bunga is surrounded by his General Adina Beg. The rivalry between Sardar Jassa Singh Ji (Ahluwalia Misl) and Sardar Jassa Singh Ji (Ramgarhia Misl) causes the Ramgarhia Misl to form an alliance with the Mughals in an attempt to take control of the Ramrauni Bunga. However, after hearing the plight of the 500 Sikhs stranded within the Bunga, Sardar Jassa Singh Ji (Ramgarhia Misl) abandons Adina Beg's forces and rejoins the Khalsa Army.

# Second Afghan Invasion Of India

ਭਾਰਤ ਉਤੇ ਦੂਜਾ ਅਫ਼ਗਾਨੀ ਹਮਲਾ

1748 - 1749: Second Afghan Invasion of India under the command of Ahmad Shah Abdali to plunder and pillage the subcontinent.

# Third Afghan Invasion Of India

ਭਾਰਤ ਉਤੇ ਤੀਜਾ ਅਫ਼ਗ਼ਾਨੀ ਹਮਲਾ

1751 - 1752: Third Afghan Invasion of India under the command of Ahmad Shah Abdali to plunder and pillage the subcontinent. Bhai Sukha Singh Ji (who assassinated Masa Ranghar in 1740) and the Khalsa warriors attain Shaheedi fighting Ahmad Shah Abdali's forces.

# Shaheedi Of Bhai Jai Singh Ji & Family

ਭਾਈ ਜੈ ਸਿੰਘ ਜੀ ਅਤੇ ਉਹਨਾਂ ਦੇ ਪਰਿਵਾਰ ਦੀ ਸ਼ਹੀਦੀ

1753: Bhai Jai Singh Ji attains Shaheedi after being hung upside down and having his skin peeled off for refusing to transport tobacco for the Mughal Governor Abdul Samund Khan. Bhai Jai Singh Ji's wife, Mata Dhan Kaur Ji, his sons Bhai Karaka Singh Ji and Bhai Kharak Singh Ji, and daughter-in-law Bibi Raaj Kaur Ji are rounded up and they too attain Shaheedi. Upon hearing the news, the Khalsa Army attacks the Mughal Governor.

# Reconstruction Of Ramrauni Bunga

ਰਾਮਰੌਣੀ ਬੁੰਗੇ ਦੀ ਮੁੜ ਉਸਾਰੀ

1753: Sardar Jassa Singh Ji (Ramgarhia Misl) is given the seva of reconstructing the fort of Ramrauni Bunga. The Bunga is renamed Ramgarh after additional fortifications.

# Khalsa Army Attacks Lahore

ਖ਼ਾਲਸਾ ਫੌਜ ਵੱਲੋਂ ਲਾਹੌਰ ਉਤੇ ਹਮਲਾ

1753: Upon the death of Mir Mannu, the Khalsa Army attacks Lahore to successfully free all the women and children held captive in Mir Mannu's prisons.

# Gurbilas Patshahi 10: Bhai Koer Singh Ji Kalal

ਭਾਈ ਕੋਇਰ ਸਿੰਘ ਜੀ ਕੁਲਾਲ ਵੱਲੋਂ
ਗੁਰਬਿਲਾਸ ਪਾਤਸ਼ਾਹੀ ਦਸਵੀਂ ਦਾ
ਇਤਿਹਾਸਕ ਗ੍ਰੰਥ ਲਿਖਿਆ ਗਿਆ

1754: Bhai Koer Singh Ji Kalal completes the literary work of Gurbilas Patshahi 10 containing the history of the Gurus.

# Fourth Afghan Invasion Of India

ਭਾਰਤ ਉਤੇ ਚੌਥਾ ਅਫਗਾਨੀ ਹਮਲਾ

1756 - 1757: Fourth Afghan Invasion of India under the command of Ahmad Shah Abdali to plunder and pillage the subcontinent.

# Shaheedi Of Baba Deep Singh Ji & The Khalsa Warriors

ਬਾਬਾ ਦੀਪ ਸਿੰਘ ਜੀ ਦੀ ਸ਼ਹੀਦੀ

1757: Baba Deep Singh Ji attains Shaheedi as he and the Khalsa Army free Sri Harmandir Sahib from the Afghan forces of Ahmad Shah Abdali. During the heat of battle, Baba Deep Singh Ji's head is decapitated from his body by an Afghan soldier, a fellow Sikh warrior sees this and does an Ardaas saying that Baba Ji had promised to free Sri Harmandir Sahib before becoming Shaheed. Upon doing the Ardaas, Baba Deep Singh Ji reawakens, places his severed head onto the palm of one hand and his double edged Khanda in the other; and continues fighting until the Afghan forces flee the battlefield in dread and shock at seeing a headless Singh tearing through enemy ranks. Gurdwara Baba Deep Singh Ji now stands at this site.

# Khalsa Army Avenges The Desecration Of Sri Harmandir Sahib

ਖ਼ਾਲਸਾ ਫ਼ੌਜ ਨੇ ਸ੍ਰੀ ਹਰਿਮੰਦਰ ਸਾਹਿਬ ਦੀ ਹੋਈ ਬੇਅਦਬੀ ਦਾ ਅਫ਼ਗਾਨੀਆਂ ਤੋਂ ਬਦਲਾ ਲਿਆ

1757: Sardar Jassa Singh Ji (Ahluwalia Misl) orders the Khalsa Army to avenge the desecration of Sri Harmandir Sahib and the Shaheedi of Baba Deep Singh Ji.

# Khalsa Army Avenges The Desecration Of Gurdwara Tham Sahib

ਖ਼ਾਲਸਾ ਫ਼ੌਜ ਨੇ ਗੁਰਦਵਾਰਾ ਥੰਮ ਸਾਹਿਬ ਦੀ ਹੋਈ ਬੇਅਦਬੀ ਦਾ ਮੁਗ਼ਲਾਂ ਤੋਂ ਬਦਲਾ ਲਿਆ

1757: Jahan Khan sends his Mughal forces to attack Gurdwara Tham Sahib, Kartarpur. Surviving the attack, Bibi Nirbhai Kaur Ji mounts an operation with her fiancé, Bhai Harnam Singh Ji, to rescue captive women from Jahan Khan's camp. Upon rescuing the women, Sardar Jassa Singh Ji (Ahluwalia Misl) commands the Khalsa Army to avenge the desecration of Gurdwara Tham Sahib.

# Passing Of Sufi Faqir Bulle Shah Ji

ਅਕਾਲ ਚਲਾਣਾ ਸੂਫੀ
ਫਕੀਰ ਬੁੱਲੇ ਸ਼ਾਹ ਜੀ

1757: Known for his outspoken solidarity and support for the Sikhs, Bulleh Shah Ji, a Panjabi Sufi saint and poet, passes away.

# Fifth Afghan Invasion Of India

ਭਾਰਤ ਉੱਤੇ ਪੰਜਵਾਂ ਅਫ਼ਗਾਨੀ ਹਮਲਾ

1759: Fifth Afghan Invasion of India under the command of Ahmad Shah Abdali to plunder and pillage the subcontinent.

# Gathering Of Sarbat Khalsa

## Khalsa Army Attacks Lahore

ਸਰਬੱਤ ਖ਼ਾਲਸਾ : ਖ਼ਾਲਸਾ ਫ਼ੌਜ ਵੱਲੋਂ ਲਾਹੌਰ ਉਤੇ ਹਮਲਾ

1760: Under the command of Sardar Jassa Singh Ji (Ahluwalia Misl), the Khalsa Army attacks Lahore. Leading the attack alongside Sardar Jassa Singh Ji (Ahluwalia Misl) is Sardar Hari Singh Ji (Bhangi Misl), Sardar Jai Singh Ji (Kanhaiya Misl) and Sardar Charat Singh Ji (Sukerchakia Misl and Maharaja Ranjit Singh Ji's grandfather). Knowing that the Afghans and Maharatas are currently at war, the Khalsa Army accepts a tribute of 30,000 rupees from the Afghans. The Khalsa Army strategically withdraws to let both the Afghan and Maharata Armies annihilate each other, leaving Lahore for the taking at a later time.

1761
੧੭੬੧

# Gathering of Sarbat Khalsa

## Khalsa Army Frees 22,000 Captive Women

ਸਰਬੱਤ ਖਾਲਸਾ: ਖਾਲਸਾ ਫੌਜ ਨੇ ਅਫਗਾਨੀਆਂ ਤੋਂ ਤਕਰੀਬਨ ੨੨,੦੦੦ ਹਿੰਦੂ ਕੈਦੀ ਔਰਤਾਂ ਨੂੰ ਛਡਵਾਇਆ

1761: After the Battle of Panipat where the Maharata Army is defeated by Ahmad Shah Abdali. Maharata civilians come to Sarbat Khalsa requesting the Khalsa Army to rescue around 22,000 Hindu women who are being taken back to Afghanistan to be sold as slave girls. Upon hearing this, Sardar Jassa Singh Ji (Ahluwalia Misl) leads the Khalsa Army and successfully rescues the Maharata women.

# Sixth Afghan Invasion Of India

ਭਾਰਤ ਉਤੇ ਛੇਵਾਂ ਅਫਗਾਨੀ ਹਮਲਾ

1762: Sixth Afghan Invasion of India under the command of Ahmad Shah Abdali to plunder and pillage the subcontinent.

# Afghan Attack On Sri Harmandir Sahib

ਸ੍ਰੀ ਹਰਮੰਦਰ ਸਾਹਿਬ ਉੱਤੇ ਅਫਗਾਨੀ ਹਮਲਾ

1762: Under the command of Ahmad Shah Abdali,
the Afghan Army demolishes Sri Harmandir Sahib.

# Vada Ghalughara

## The Great Genocide

ਵੱਡਾ ਘੱਲੂਘਾਰਾ ਜਿਸ ਵਿਚ ਤਕਰੀਬਨ ੩੦,੦੦੦ ਸਿੱਖ ਸ਼ਹੀਦ ਹੋਏ

1762: Vada Ghalughara, the Great Genocide. Around 30,000 Sikhs lose their lives and attain Shaheedi in the heat of survival against Ahmad Shah Abdali's forces.

1762

੧੭੬੨

# Excommunication Of Baba Ala Singh Ji

ਸ੍ਰੀ ਅਕਾਲ ਤਖ਼ਤ ਵੱਲੋਂ ਬਾਬਾ ਆਲਾ ਸਿੰਘ ਜੀ (ਫੂਲਕੀਆ ਮਿਸਲ) ਨੂੰ ਪੰਥ ਵਿੱਚੋਂ ਛੇਕਿਆ ਗਿਆ

1762: Baba Ala Singh Ji (Phulkia Misl), is excommunicated from the Khalsa Army for the reasons of; 1) his alliance with Ahmad Shah Abdali, 2) not coming to the aid of the Khalsa Army to defend against the attack of Ahmad Shah Abdali's forces during the Vada Ghalughara.

# 1762 *to* 1799

## KHALSA MISL RAAJ

ਖ਼ਾਲਸਾ ਮਿਸਲਾਂ ਦਾ ਰਾਜ

# CONTENTS

## KHALSA MISL RAAJ

With the Mughals, Afghans and Persians feeling diminished and exhausted by the fighting spirit of the Sikhs, the Khalsa Army begins to establish its sovereign right to the self-determination of Panjab.

With the Panjab now securely in the hands of the Guru's Army, the Khalsa Misls now have the throne of the Delhi in their sight as they begin expanding their territories beyond Panjab. Making several incursions on the royal seat of India, the Sikhs are able to raise the Nishan of the Khalsa over Delhi on numerous occasions, bringing forth a new power upon the Indian subcontinent.

# Khalsa Army Attains The Zamzama Canon

ਖ਼ਾਲਸਾ ਫ਼ੌਜ ਨੇ ਅਫ਼ਗ਼ਾਨੀ ਫ਼ੌਜ ਤੋਂ
ਜ਼ਮਜ਼ਮਾ ਤੋਪ ਹਾਸਲ ਕਰ ਲਈ

1762: The Khalsa Army under the command of Sardar Hari Singh Ji (Bhangi Misl) takes possession of Ahmad Shah Abdali's famed Zamzama canon and renames the canon the Bhangi Toap.

# Khalsa Army Begins Taking Over Panjab

ਖ਼ਾਲਸਾ ਫ਼ੌਜ ਵੱਲੋਂ ਪੰਜਾਬ ਉਤੇ ਆਪਣੇ ਰਾਜ ਦੀ ਸ਼ੁਰੂਆਤ

1763: As Ahmad Shah Abdali's Afghan forces become restricted to their encampments, Sardar Hari Singh Ji (Bhangi Misl) takes control of Kasur, in present day Panjab, Pakistan. Sardar Jassa Singh Ji (Ahluwalia Misl) retakes the Jallandhar Doab, as well as taking the city of Morinda after defeating Bhikan Khan of Malerkotla. Sardar Charat Singh Ji (Sukerchakia Misl and Maharaja Ranjit Singh Ji's grandfather) along with Sardar Hari Singh Ji (Bhangi Misl) take Sialkot after defeating General Jahan Khan of the Afghan forces, in present day Panjab, Pakistan.

# Khalsa Army Retakes Sirhind

ਖ਼ਾਲਸਾ ਫ਼ੌਜ ਦੀ ਦੁਬਾਰਾ ਸਰਹੰਦ
ਉਤੇ ਫਤਿਹ

1764: Under the command of Sardar Jassa Singh Ji (Ahluwalia Misl), the Khalsa Army retakes the city of Sirhind and begins the construction of Gurdwara Fatehgarh Sahib at the site of Sahibzada Zorawar Singh Ji and Sahibzada Fateh Singh Ji's Shaheedi.

# Seventh Afghan Invasion Of India

ਭਾਰਤ ਉਤੇ ਸਤਵਾਂ ਅਫਗਾਨੀ ਹਮਲਾ

1764: Seventh Afghan Invasion of India under the command of Ahmad Shah Abdali to plunder and pillage the subcontinent.

# Shaheedi Of Baba Gurbaksh Singh Ji & The Khalsa Warriors

ਬਾਬਾ ਗੁਰਬੱਖਸ਼ ਸਿੰਘ ਜੀ ਦੀ ਸ਼ਹੀਦੀ

1764: Baba Gurbaksh Singh Ji and 29 of his Singhs attain Shaheedi defending Sri Harmandir Sahib from 30,000 troops of Ahmad Shah Abdali's forces.

1764

੧੭੬੪

# Khalsa Army Takes Saharnpur & Najibad

ਖਾਲਸਾ ਫੋਜ ਦੀ ਸਹਾਰਨਪੁਰ ਅਤੇ ਨਾਜੀਬਾਦ ਉਤੇ ਫਤਾਹ

1764: Under the command of Sardar Baghel Singh Ji (Karora Singhia Misl), 40,000 warriors of the Khalsa Army capture the city of Saharnpur and Najibad in present day Uttar Pradesh from Ruhila Chief Najib ud-Daulah. Sardar Baghel Singh Ji (Karora Singhia Misl) charges Najib ud-Daula an annual tax of eleven lakh (RS 1,100,000) rupees in order for him to keep his Kingdom.

# Reconstruction Of Sri Harmandir Sahib

ਸ੍ਰੀ ਹਰਮੰਦਰ ਸਾਹਿਬ ਦੀ ਦੁਬਾਰਾ ਉਸਾਰੀ

1765: Khalsa Army begins reconstructing the complex of Sri Harmandir Sahib after forcing Ahmad Shah Abdali to retreat once again from India.

# Khalsa Army Retakes Lahore

ਖ਼ਾਲਸਾ ਫ਼ੌਜ ਦੀ ਦੁਬਾਰਾ ਲਾਹੌਰ ਉਤੇ ਫਤਹਿ

1765: Under the command of Sardar Gajjar Singh Ji and Sardar Lehna Singh Ji (Bhangi Misl), the Khalsa Army retakes the city of Lahore from the Afghan forces of Ahmad Shah Abdali.

# Eighth Afghan Invasion Of India

ਭਾਰਤ ਉਤੇ ਅਠਵਾਂ ਅਫਗਾਨੀ ਹਮਲਾ

1766: Eighth Afghan Invasion of India under the command of Ahmad Shah Abdali to plunder and pillage the subcontinent.

# Khalsa Army Has Full Control Over Panjab

ਖ਼ਾਲਸਾ ਫ਼ੌਜ ਦਾ ਪੰਜਾਬ ਉਤੇ ਪੂਰਾ ਰਾਜ ਪ੍ਰਬੰਧ

1767: Khalsa Army has now taken over the whole of Panjab.

# Ninth Afghan Invasion Of India

ਭਾਰਤ ਉਤੇ ਨੌਵਾਂ ਅਫਗਾਨੀ ਹਮਲਾ

1769: Ninth Afghan Invasion of India under the command of Ahmad Shah Abdali to plunder and pillage the subcontinent.

1770

੧੭੭੦

# Khalsa Misls Begin Expanding Their Territories

ਖ਼ਾਲਸਾ ਮਿਸਲਾਂ ਨੇ ਆਪੋ–ਆਪਣਾ
ਰਾਜ ਵਧਾਉਣਾ ਸ਼ੁਰੂ ਕਰ ਦਿਤਾ

1770: Khalsa Misls begin expanding their own individual territories at the expense of fighting one another. However, during times when Panjab is under threat of attack from an external enemy, the Misls regroup, setting aside their differences, to come to Panjab's defence as a single military unit.

1773

੧੭੭੩

# Khalsa Army
# Takes Delhi

ਖ਼ਾਲਸਾ ਫ਼ੌਜ ਦੀਆਂ ਕਰੋੜ
ਸਿੰਘੀਆ ਅਤੇ ਡੂਲਕੀਆ ਸਿਮਲਾਂ
ਵੱਲੋਂ ਦਿੱਲੀ ਉਤੇ ਫਤਿਹ

1773: Under the command of Sardar Baghel Singh Ji (Karora Singhia Misl), the Khalsa Army take Delhi. The Mughal Emperor Shah Alam II is now in disarray as to what to do. Shah Alam II at first attempts to buy out the Sikhs by offering employment, but after this is unsuccessful Shah Alam II enlists the help of Abdul Ahad Khan and Walter Reinhardt Sombre, a German mercenary working for the Mughal court. Both Abdul Ahad Khan and Walter Reinhardt Sombre are defeated by the Sikhs and the Khalsa Army returns once again to take Delhi. Najaf Khan and Mullah Rahim Dad Khan are recruited in the next round of attacks on the Sikhs, but under the command of Sardar Amar Singh Ji and Sardar Gajpat Singh Ji (Phulkia Misl), Mullah Rahim Dad Khan is killed in battle and Najaf Khan is forced to surrender.

# Khalsa Army Takes Delhi

ਖ਼ਾਲਸਾ ਫ਼ੌਜ ਦੀਆਂ ਕਰੋੜ
ਸਿੰਘੀਆ, ਭੰਗੀ ਅਤੇ
ਧਾਲੇਵਾਲੀਆ ਮਿਸਲਾਂ ਵੱਲੋਂ
ਦਿੱਲੀ ਉਤੇ ਫਤੇਹ

1775: Under the command of Sardar Baghel Singh Ji (Karora Singhia Misl), Sardar Rai Singh Ji (Bhangi Misl) and Sardar Tara Singh Ji (Dallewalia Misl), the Khalsa Army launches another attack on Delhi, expanding further into the present day city of New Delhi.

# Khalsa Army Takes The Yamuna Gangetic Doab

ਖ਼ਾਲਸਾ ਫ਼ੋਜ ਦੀ ਕਰੋੜ ਸਿੰਘੀਆ ਮਿਸਲ ਵੱਲੋਂ ਜਮੁਨਾ ਅਤੇ ਗੰਗਾ ਦੁਆਬ ਉਤੇ ਫਤਹਿ

1776: Under the command of Sardar Baghel Singh Ji (Karora Singhia Misl), the Khalsa Army defeats the Mughal forces of Shah Alam II near Muzaffarnagar in present day Uttar Pradesh. The entire area of the Yamuna Gangetic Doab of present day Uttar Pradesh is now under the control of the Khalsa Army.

# Mughal Army Surrenders To The Khalsa

ਮੁਗਲ ਫੌਜ ਵੱਲੋਂ ਖਾਲਸਾ ਫੌਜ
ਦੀ ਕਰੋੜ ਸਿੰਘੀਆ ਸਿਸਲ ਅਗੇ
ਆਤਮ ਸਮਰਪਣ

1778: Mughal Emperor Shah Alam II sends a force of 100,000 Mughal soldiers to attack Sardar Baghel Singh Ji (Karora Singhia Misl) and the Khalsa Army at the Battle of Ghanaur near present day Patiala, Panjab. Sardar Baghel Singh Ji (Karora Singhia Misl) is able to outmanoeuvre the Mughal forces, leading to the surrender of Wazir Nawab Maja ud Daula and the Mughal Army.

# Khalsa Misls Unite Against The Mughal Army

ਮੁਗਲ ਫੌਜ ਦੇ ਖਿਲਾਫ, ਖਾਲਸਾ ਫੌਜ ਦੀ ਕਰੋੜ ਸਿੰਘੀਆ ਅਤੇ ਫੁਲਕੀਆ ਸਿਸਲਾਂ ਦੀ ਇਕਜੁਟਤਾ

1779: Sardar Baghel Singh Ji (Karora Singhia Misl), Sardar Rai Singh Ji of Buna and Sardar Bhanga Singh Ji of Thanesar form a temporary alliance with the Mughal forces of Prince Farkhanda Bakht and Wazir Abdul Ahad Khan. The combined force surrounds the cis-Sutlej states of the Phulkia Misl in present day Patiala, Panjab. However, Sardar Amar Singh Ji (Phulkia Misl) is able to come to terms of peace with Sardar Baghel Singh Ji (Karora Singhia Misl) by asking that his son, Bhai Sahib Singh Ji, take Amrit at the hands of the Panj Pyare of which Sardar Baghel Singh Ji (Karora Singhia Misl) is a part of. The combined force Karora Singhia Misl and Phulkia Misl unite to turn on the surrounding Mughals. Prince Farkhanda Bakht and Wazir Abdul Ahad Khan and their Mughal troops flee in desperation after seeing that the Khalsa Misls have joined forces against the Mughals.

1781

ੴ੮੧

# Khalsa Army Retaliates To Attacks Made On Its Military Posts

ਮੁਗਲ ਫੌਜ ਵੱਲੋਂ ਖਾਲਸਾ ਫੌਜ ਦੀਆਂ ਛਾਉਣੀਆਂ ਉਤੇ ਹਮਲੇ ਦਾ ਬਦਲਾ, ਕਰੋੜ ਸਿੰਘੀਆ ਮਿਸਲ ਵੱਲੋਂ ਲਿਆ ਗਿਆ

1781: Mirza Shafi, a close relative of the Mughal Prime Minister, captures the Sikh military post at Indri in present day Haryana. Sardar Baghel Singh Ji (Karora Singhia Misl) retaliates by attacking Khalil Beg Khan of Shahabad who surrenders 300 horses and 2 cannons to the Khalsa Army.

੧੭੮੩

# Khalsa Army Takes Delhi

ਖ਼ਾਲਸਾ ਫ਼ੌਜ ਦੀਆਂ ਕਰੋੜ ਸਿੰਘੀਆ, ਆਹਲੂਵਾਲੀਆ ਅਤੇ ਰਾਮਗੜ੍ਹੀਆ ਮਿਸਲਾਂ ਵੱਲੋਂ ਦਿੱਲੀ ਉਤੇ ਫਤਹਿ

1783: Under the command of Sardar Baghel Singh Ji (Karora Singhia Misl), Sardar Jassa Singh Ji (Ahluwalia Misl) and Sardar Jassa Singh Ji (Ramgarhia Misl), the Khalsa Army takes control of Delhi. Shah Alam II surrenders as Sardar Baghel Singh Ji (Karora Singhia Misl) orders the building of historical Gurdwaras in memory of Sri Guru Harkrishan Ji and Sri Guru Tegh Bahadur Ji. The Gurdwaras are funded by taxing the trade at a rate of 37.5% which flows in and out of Delhi as Sardar Baghel Singh Ji (Karora Singhia Misl) does not wish to have any Mughal state finances involved in the construction of the Gurdwaras. Upon leaving Delhi, the Khalsa Army chains up the foundation of the throne of Delhi and drags it back to Amritsar as a prisoner of war.

# Khalsa Army Takes Delhi

ਖ਼ਾਲਸਾ ਫ਼ੌਜ ਦੀ ਕਰੋੜ ਸਿੰਘੀਆ
ਮਿਸਲ ਵੱਲੋਂ ਦਿੱਲੀ ਉਤੇ ਫ਼ਤਾਹ

1785: Sardar Baghel Singh Ji (Karora Singhia Misl) decides to attack Delhi once again. Shah Alam II, afraid of the Khalsa Army, signs a treaty with the Maharatas. The Maharatas initiate an agreement with Sardar Baghel Singh Ji (Karora Singhia Misl) and consent to pay 1,000,000 rupees as a gift.

# Shaheedi Of Sardarni Shamsher Kaur Ji & The Khalsa Warriors

ਸਰਦਾਰਨੀ ਸਮਸ਼ੇਰ ਕੌਰ ਜੀ ਦੀ ਸ਼ਹੀਦੀ

1785: Sardarni Shamsher Kaur Ji is given command over five villages near Hansi by Sardar Jassa Singh Ji (Ramgarhia Misl). She later attains Shaheedi along with 1,000 Khalsa warriors defending her fort from an army of Maharatas numbering the thousands.

# Sardarni Sada Kaur Ji Brings About Peace Between The Sukerchakia & Kanhaiya Misls

ਸਰਦਾਰਨੀ ਸਦਾ ਕੌਰ ਜੀ ਨੇ ਸੁਕਰਚੱਕੀਆ ਅਤੇ ਘਨੱਈਆ ਮਿਸਲਾਂ ਵਿਚਕਾਰ ਸਮਝੌਤਾ ਕਰਵਾਉਣਾ

1786: Sardar Maha Singh Ji (Sukerchakia Misl, and the father of Maharaja Ranjit Singh Ji) and Sardar Jassa Singh Ji (Ramgarhia Misl) form an alliance to attack Sardar Gurbaksh Singh Ji (Kanhaiya Misl), resulting in Sardar Gurbaksh Singh Ji's (Kanhaiya Misl) death on the battlefield. Seeing the destructive situation of the Khalsa Misls fighting one another, Sardarni Sada Kaur Ji, the daughter-in-law of the Kanhaiya Misl, requests that her daughter, Rani Mehtab Kaur Ji, be engaged to Sardar Ranjit Singh Ji (Sukerchakia Misl) in order to begin bringing about peace and unity between the warring Misls.

# The Command of Sardarni Sada Kaur Ji

ਸਰਦਾਰਨੀ ਸਦਾ ਕੌਰ ਜੀ ਨੇ
ਅਹਲੂਈਆ ਮਿਸਲ ਦੀ ਕਮਾਨ
ਸੰਭਾਲਣੀ

1789: Sardarni Sada Kaur Ji becomes the head of the Kanhaiya Misl, taking charge of 8,000 cavalry warriors.

# Guru Kian Sakhian

ਭਾਈ ਸਵਰੂਪ ਸਿੰਘ ਜੀ
ਵੱਲੋਂ ਗੁਰੂ ਕੀਆਂ ਸਾਖੀਆਂ
ਦਾ ਇਤਿਹਾਸਕ ਗ੍ਰੰਥ
ਲਿਖਿਆ ਗਿਆ

1790: Bhai Svaroop Singh Ji completes the literary work of Guru Kian Sakhian containing the history of the Gurus.

# The Command of Sardar Ranjit Singh Ji

ਸਰਦਾਰ ਰਣਜੀਤ ਸਿੰਘ ਜੀ ਨੇ ਸ਼ੁਕਰਚੱਕੀਆ ਮਿਸਲ ਦੀ ਕਮਾਨ ਸੰਭਾਲਣੀ

1792: Sardar Ranjit Singh Ji becomes head of the Sukerchakia Misl. As his mother-in-law to be, Sardarni Sada Kaur Ji (Kanhaiya Misl) becomes Sardar Ranjit Singh Ji's regent and begins advising him on how to unify the Khalsa Misls again into one single fighting force.

# Maharata Army Suffers Heavy Losses At The Hands Of The Khalsa

ਖਾਲਸਾ ਫੌਜ ਦੀ ਡੁਲਕੀਆ ਸਿਮਲ ਵੱਲੋਂ
ਮਰਾਨਾ ਫੌਜ ਦਾ ਭਾਰੀ ਨੁਕਸਾਨ

1794: Holding the office of Prime Minister for the Phulkia Misl, Sardarni Sahib Kaur Ji leads a force of 7,000 Khalsa warriors into battle to defend the Sutlej states in present day Patiala, Panjab from an attack by a Maharata force of 100,000 led by Anta Rao and Lachhman Rao. The Phulkia Misl is able to defeat the stronger force of the Maharatas, with the Khalsa suffering a loss of a third of its warriors whilst the Maharata Army suffers heavier losses of half of their forces.

# Khalsa Army Defends India From A Final Afghan Invasion

ਖ਼ਾਲਸਾ ਫ਼ੌਜ ਵੱਲੋਂ, ਅਫ਼ਗ਼ਾਨੀ ਫ਼ੌਜ ਦੇ ਭਾਰਤ ਉਤੇ ਕੀਤੇ ਅਖ਼ੀਰਲੇ ਹਮਲੇ ਦਾ ਟਾਕਰਾ

1796 - 1798: Shah Zaman of Afghanistan attempts an invasion of India. Sardar Ranjit Singh Ji (Sukerchakia Misl) persuades the Khalsa Misls to remain and fight. Under Sardar Ranjit Singh Ji's (Sukerchakia Misl) leadership the invasion of the Afghans is repelled.

1797

੧੭੯੭

# Gurbilas Patshahi 10

## Giani Sukha Singh Ji

ਗਿਆਨੀ ਸੁੱਖਾ ਸਿੰਘ ਜੀ ਵੱਲੋਂ ਗੁਰਬਿਲਾਸ
ਪਾਤਸ਼ਾਹੀ ਦਸਵੀਂ ਦਾ ਇਤਿਹਾਸਕ ਗ੍ਰੰਥ
ਲਿਖਿਆ ਗਿਆ

1797: Giani Sukha Singh Ji completes the literary work of Gurbilas Patshahi 10 detailing the history of Sri Guru Gobind Singh Ji.

# Khalsa Army Frees The State Of Jind

ਖਾਲਸਾ ਫੌਜ ਦੀ ਡੁਲਕੀਆ ਮਿਸਲ ਵੱਲੋਂ ਜਿੰਦ ਦਾ ਇਲਾਕਾ ਆਜ਼ਾਦ ਕਰਵਾਇਆ ਗਿਆ

1799: Sardarni Sahib Kaur Ji (Phulkia Misl) commands a force of 9,000 Khalsa warriors to attack the strongholdings of George Thomas, an independent Irish adventurer who ruled Hansi, in order to free the State of Jind from a siege by Thomas.

# Sardar Ranjit Singh Ji Moves To Take Control Of Panjab

ਸਰਦਾਰ ਰਣਜੀਤ ਸਿੰਘ ਜੀ
(ਸ਼ੁਕਰਚੱਕੀਆ ਮਿਸਲ) ਵੱਲੋਂ ਪੂਰੇ
ਪੰਜਾਬ ਉੱਤੇ ਆਪਣਾ ਰਾਜਭਾਗ
ਕਾਇਮ ਕਰਨ ਦੀ ਆਰੰਭਤਾ

1799: Under the guidance of Sardarni Sada Kaur Ji (Kanhaiya Misl), Sardar Ranjit Singh Ji (Sukerchakia Misl) is advised to attack Lahore in an attempt to control Panjab as a whole.

# 1801 to 1843

## MAHARAJA RANJIT SINGH JI'S RAAJ

ਮਾਹਾਰਾਜਾ ਰਣਜੀਤ ਸਿੰਘ ਜੀ ਦਾ ਰਾਜ

# CONTENTS

## MAHARAJA RANJIT SINGH JI'S RAAJ

As the Khalsa Misls enjoy the pleasures of their own individual states, under the guidance of Sardarni Sada Kaur Ji, Maharaja Ranjit Singh Ji takes it upon himself to begin consolidating the confederacy of the Khalsa Misls into a single and unified Nation.

Forming alliances with some Khalsa Misls whilst overpowering others, Maharaja Ranjit Singh Ji is able to bring together the Sikhs of Panjab and unite them under the Kingdom of Panjab.

With peace now fully restored and the territory of Panjab expanding rapidly towards Afghanistan and China, the Kingdom of Panjab experiences economic growth and prosperity which leaves it on par with some of the richest Nations of the world during the early 19th century.

# Sardar Ranjit Singh Ji Crowned As Maharaja Ranjit Singh Ji

ਸਰਦਾਰ ਰਣਜੀਤ ਸਿੰਘ ਜੀ ਨੂੰ ਪੰਜਾਬ ਦਾ ਮਾਹਾਰਾਜਾ ਹੋਣ ਦਾ ਖਿਤਾਬ

1801: Baba Sahib Singh Ji Bedi of Sri Guru Nanak Dev Ji's lineage coronates Sardar Ranjit Singh Ji (Sukerchakia Misl) as Maharaja Ranjit Singh Ji, the new Sovereign of Panjab. Sardarni Sada Kaur Ji (Kanhaiya Misl) continues to provide strategic insight to assist Maharaja Ranjit Singh Ji in expanding the Panjab Empire.

# Sukerchakia & Ahluwalia Misls Unite

ਸੁਕਰਚੱਕੀਆ ਅਤੇ ਆਹਲੂਵਾਲੀਆ ਮਿਸਲਾਂ ਵਿਚਕਾਰ ਆਪਸੀ ਸਮਝੌਤਾ

1802: Maharaja Ranjit Singh Ji's Sukerchakia Misl forms an alliance with the Ahluwalia Misl, now being led by Sardar Fateh Singh Ji Ahluwalia (grand-nephew of Sardar Jassa Singh Ji Ahluwalia), in order to unify Panjab as a Sovereign State.

# Akali Phula Singh Ji & Sardar Jodh Singh Ji (Ramgarhia Misl) Both Join Maharaja Ranjit Singh Ji

ਅਕਾਲੀ ਫੂਲਾ ਸਿੰਘ ਜੀ ਦੀ ਨਿਹੰਗ ਫੌਜ ਅਤੇ ਸਰਦਾਰ ਜੋਧ ਸਿੰਘ ਜੀ (ਰਾਮਗੜ੍ਹੀਆ ਮਿਸਲ) ਦਾ ਮਾਹਾਰਾਜਾ ਰਣਜੀਤ ਸਿੰਘ ਜੀ ਦੇ ਨਾਲ ਸਮਝੌਤਾ

1802: Maharaja Ranjit Singh Ji takes control of Amritsar. Akali Phula Singh Ji and his Khalsa warriors join Maharaja Ranjit Singh Ji's Army. Sardar Jodh Singh Ji Ramgarhia (son of Sardar Jassa Singh Ji Ramgarhia) also joins Maharaja Ranjit Singh Ji's forces and begins the task of building the first two storeys of Gurdwara Baba Atal Sahib.

# First Treaty Between The Sikhs & The British

ਸਿੱਖਾਂ ਅਤੇ ਅੰਗਰੇਜਾਂ ਵਿਚਕਾਰ ਪਹਿਲੀ ਸੰਧੀ

1806: The First Treaty is signed between Maharaja Ranjit Singh Ji and the British, outlining an agreement of friendship between the Sikhs and the East India Company.

# The Supreme Command Of Akali Phula Singh Ji

ਅਕਾਲੀ ਫੂਲਾ ਸਿੰਘ ਜੀ ਨੂੰ
ਅਕਾਲ ਤਖਤ ਦਾ ਮੁਖੀ ਸਥਾਪਤ
ਕੀਤਾ ਗਿਆ

1807: Akali Phula Singh Ji becomes Mukhi, Supreme Leader, of Sri Akal Takht.

# The Treaty Of Amritsar Between The Sikhs & British

ਸਿੱਖਾਂ ਅਤੇ ਅੰਗਰੇਜਾ ਵਿਚਕਾਰ ਅੰਮ੍ਰਿਤਸਰ ਦੀ ਸੰਧੀ

1809: The Treaty of Amritsar is signed with the British, in an attempt by the British to prevent Maharaja Ranjit Singh Ji from expanding his empire towards the territory of the East India Company.

# Khalsa Army
# Takes Attock

ਖਾਲਸਾ ਫੌਜ ਦੀ ਅਟਕ ਉਤੇ ਫਤਹਿ

1813: Battle of Attock. The Khalsa Army, under the command of Maharaja Ranjit Singh Ji, Sardar Hari Singh Ji Nalwa and Akali Phula Singh Ji, takes control of Attock from the Durrani Empire, which ruled present day Iran, Afghanistan and Pakistan. The head nurse, Bibi Prem Kaur Ji attains Shaheedi after igniting an Afghan ammunition bunker, causing a huge explosion within the Afghan ranks, allowing for the Khalsa Army to defeat the Afghan forces.

1813

ੴ੧੩

# Afghan Hand Over Of The Koh-I-Noor

ਅਫਗਾਨਾ ਵੱਲੋਂ ਮਹਾਰਾਜਾ ਰਣਜੀਤ ਸਿੰਘ ਜੀ ਨੂੰ ਕੋਹੇਨੂਰ ਹੀਰਾ ਸੌਂਪ ਦਿੱਤਾ ਗਿਆ

1813: The Afghan's hand over the Koh-i-noor diamond to Maharaja Ranjit Singh Ji.

# Khalsa Army
# Takes Kashmir

ਖਾਲਸਾ ਫੌਜ ਦੀ ਕਸ਼ਮੀਰ ਉਤੇ
ਚੜਾਈ

1819: The Khalsa Army marches on Kashmir. In ending five centuries of Muslim rule, Kashmir now becomes part of Panjab. Sardar Hari Singh Ji Nalwa is appointed Governor of Kashmir.

# Renovation Of Sri Nankana Sahib

ਸ੍ਰੀ ਨਨਕਾਣਾ ਸਾਹਿਬ ਦੀ ਮੁਰੰਮਤ

1820: Maharaja Ranjit Singh Ji commands the Ramgarhia Misl to oversee the renovation work of Gurdwara Sri Nankana Sahib, the birthplace of Sri Guru Nanak Dev Ji. The much needed work allows for the humble looking building to be transformed into a palace like structure.

1821

ੴ੨੧

# Arrest Of Sardarni Sada Kaur Ji

ਸਰਦਾਰਨੀ ਸਦਾ ਕੌਰ ਜੀ ਦੀ ਗ੍ਰਿਫ਼ਤਾਰੀ

1821: After taking on a second wife and marrying Rani Datar Kaur Ji (Nakai Misl), Maharaja Ranjit Singh Ji's relations with his first wife, Maharani Mehtab Kaur Ji (Kanhaiya Misl), begin to turn sour, resulting in a breakdown of Maharaja Ranjit Singh Ji's relationship with his mother in-law, Sardarni Sada Kaur Ji (Kanhaiya Misl). Upon Maharaja Ranjit Singh Ji's declaration of an heir apparent from his second marriage, Sardarni Sada Kaur Ji (Kanhaiya Misl) begins focusing her ambitions on creating a sovereign state in her own right. This leads to tensions which ultimately cause Maharaja Ranjit Singh Ji to take possession of Sardarni Sada Kaur Ji's (Kanhaiya Misl) estate and assets; and to put the 70 year old Sardarni under arrest until her passing in 1832.

# Europeanisation Of The Khalsa Army

ਖ਼ਾਲਸਾ ਫੌਜ ਨੂੰ ਫਰਾਂਸ ਅਤੇ ਇਟਲੀ ਦੇ ਜੰਗੀ ਜਰਨੈਲਾਂ ਵੱਲੋਂ ਸਿਖਲਾਈ ਦਿਤੀ ਗਈ

1822: Europeanisation of Maharaja Ranjit Singh Ji's Army under the command of French and Italian Generals, Jean-François Allard and Jean-Baptiste Ventura. European methods of war and organisation are implemented into the Khalsa Army.

# Shaheedi Of Akali Phula Singh Ji

ਅਕਾਲੀ ਫੂਲਾ ਸਿੰਘ ਜੀ ਦੀ ਸ਼ਹੀਦੀ

1823: Akali Phula Singh Ji attains Shaheedi in the Battle of Peshawar. Akali Hanuman Singh Ji is appointed Mukhi, Supreme Leader, of Sri Akal Takht.

# Gold Plating Of Sri Harmandir Sahib

ਸ੍ਰੀ ਹਰਮੰਦਰ ਸਾਹਿਬ ਉਤੇ ਸੋਨੇ ਦੀ ਸੇਵਾ

1830: The gold plating of Sri Harmandir Sahib is completed as commissioned by Maharaja Ranjit Singh Ji.

1832

੧੮੩੨

# Construction Of Takht Sri Hazur Sahib

ਤਖ਼ਤ ਸ੍ਰੀ ਹਜ਼ੂਰ ਸਾਹਿਬ ਦੀ ਉਸਾਰੀ

1832 - 1837: Maharaja Ranjit Singh Ji commissions the building of Takht Sri Hazur Sahib, which later becomes one of the Five Thrones of the Sikh Nation.

# Khalsa Army
# Takes Ladakh

ਖ਼ਾਲਸਾ ਫ਼ੌਜ ਦੀ ਲਦਾਖ਼ ਉਤੇ
ਫਤਿਹ

1836: Sardar Zorawar Singh Ji Kahluria secures control over Ladakh, allowing for Maharaja Ranjit Singh Ji to expand the Kingdom of Panjab towards the Chinese frontier.

# Khalsa Army Takes The Khyber Pass

ਖ਼ਾਲਸਾ ਫ਼ੌਜ ਦੀ ਖ਼ਾਈਬਰ ਉਤੇ ਫਤਹਿ

1836: Sardar Hari Singh Ji Nalwa secures control over the Khyber Pass. Expanding the Kingdom of Panjab towards the Afghan frontier, enabling the Khalsa Army to seal Panjab off from outside invaders. Under Sardar Hari Singh Ji Nalwa's command, Bibi Sharan Kaur Ji is tasked with gathering intelligence on Pathan forces in the surrounding areas. Undertaking one particular mission, Bibi Sharan Kaur Ji disguises herself as a Pathan woman and meets with a Pathan Chief. After acquiring the information she needs, Bibi Sharan Kaur Ji poisons the Chief unconscious with her handkerchief and assassinates him. She comes back to Sardar Hari Singh Ji Nalwa with the necessary intelligence and the mission completed.

# British Begin Arresting French & Italian Officers Looking To Join The Khalsa Army

ਅੰਗਰੇਜਾਂ ਨੇ ਖਾਲਸਾ ਫੌਜ ਵਿਚ, ਭਰਤੀ ਹੋਣ ਜਾ ਰਹੇ ਫਰਾਂਸ ਅਤੇ ਇਟਲੀ ਦੇ ਅਧਿਕਾਰੀਆਂ ਨੂੰ ਗ੍ਰਿਫਤਾਰ ਕਰਨਾ ਸ਼ੁਰੂ ਕਰ ਦਿੱਤਾ

1837: Fearing Maharaja Ranjit Singh Ji's dominance, British Authorities issue a warrant for the arrest of any French and Italian officers travelling in disguise to join the Khalsa Army.

# Shaheedi Of Sardar Hari Singh Ji Nalwa

ਸਰਦਾਰ ਹਰੀ ਸਿੰਘ ਜੀ ਨਲਵਾ ਦੀ ਸ਼ਹੀਦੀ

1837: Sardar Hari Singh Ji Nalwa attains Shaheedi in the Battle of Jamrud.

# Bibi Sharan Kaur Ji Calls In Khalsa Reinforcements

ਬੀਬੀ ਸ਼ਰਨ ਕੌਰ ਜੀ ਨੇ ਭੇਸ ਬਦਲ ਕੇ, ਮਾਹਾਰਾਜਾ ਰਣਜੀਤ ਸਿੰਘ ਜੀ ਨੂੰ, ਹੋਰ ਫੌਜਾਂ ਭੇਜਣ ਦਾ ਸਨੇਹਾ ਦਿੱਤਾ

1837: Upon the Shaheedi of Sardar Hari Singh Ji Nalwa, Bibi Sharan Kaur Ji, a spy from Sardar Hari Singh Ji Nalwa's Regiment undertakes a mission to sneak out of the surrounded fort disguised as a Pathan woman, in order to alert Khalsa reinforcements. After trekking past Pathan forces under the cover of night, Bibi Sharan Kaur Ji reaches Lahore from where she returns to the battle with Maharaja Ranjit Singh Ji and the Khalsa Army.

# Rebuilding Of Takht Sri Patna Sahib

ਤਖਤ ਸ੍ਰੀ ਪਟਨਾ ਸਾਹਿਬ ਦੀ ਦੁਬਾਰਾ ਉਸਾਰੀ

1837: Maharaja Ranjit Singh Ji commissions the rebuilding of Takht Sri Patna Sahib.

# Passing Of Maharaja Ranjit Singh Ji & Kingship Of Maharaja Kharak Singh Ji

ਮਾਹਾਰਾਜਾ ਰਣਜੀਤ ਸਿੰਘ ਜੀ ਦੇ ਅਕਾਲ ਚਲਾਣੇ ਤੋਂ ਬਾਅਦ, ਸਰਦਾਰ ਖੜਕ ਸਿੰਘ ਜੀ ਨੂੰ ਪੰਜਾਬ ਦਾ ਨਵਾਂ ਮਾਹਾਰਾਜਾ ਨੀਅਤ ਕੀਤਾ ਗਿਆ

1839: Maharaja Ranjit Singh Ji passes away in his sleep due to health complications and a stroke. His son, Maharaja Kharak Singh Ji, is installed as the new Sovereign of Panjab.

# Kingship Of Maharaja Noa Nihaal Singh Ji

ਡੋਗਰਿਆਂ ਦੀ ਗ਼ਦਾਰੀ ਕਾਰਨ, ਮਾਹਾਰਾਜਾ ਖੜਕ ਸਿੰਘ ਜੀ ਨੂੰ ਗ੍ਰਿਫਤਾਰ ਕਰਕੇ, ਸਰਦਾਰ ਨੌਨਿਹਾਲ ਸਿੰਘ ਜੀ ਨੂੰ ਪੰਜਾਬ ਦਾ ਨਵਾਂ ਮਾਹਾਰਾਜਾ ਨੀਅਤ ਕਰ ਦਿੱਤਾ ਗਿਆ

1839: After the arrest of Maharaja Kharak Singh Ji by Dogra elements who were conspiring against the Kingdom of Panjab, Maharaja Ranjit Singh Ji's grandson, Maharaja Noa Nihaal Singh Ji, is installed as the new Sovereign of Panjab.

# Queenship Of Maharani Chand Kaur Ji

ਮਾਹਾਰਾਜਾ ਨੌਨਿਹਾਲ ਸਿੰਘ ਜੀ ਦੀ ਝੁੱਕੀ ਮੌਤ ਤੋਂ ਬਾਅਦ, ਡੋਗਰਿਆਂ ਨੇ ਸਰਦਾਰਨੀ ਚੰਦ ਕੌਰ ਜੀ ਨੂੰ, ਪੰਜਾਬ ਦੀ ਨਵੀਂ ਮਾਹਾਂਰਾਣੀ ਨੀਅਤ ਕਰ ਦਿੱਤਾ

1840: After the suspicious death of Maharaja Noa Nihaal Singh Ji, Maharani Chand Kaur Ji, (Maharaja Kharak Singh Ji's wife), is installed as the new Sovereign of Panjab.

# Kingship Of Maharaja Sher Singh Ji

ਸਰਦਾਰ ਸ਼ੇਰ ਸਿੰਘ ਜੀ ਨੇ ਆਪਣੀ ਫੌਜੀ ਤਾਕਤ ਨਾਲ, ਮਾਹਾਂਰਾਣੀ ਚੰਦ ਕੌਰ ਜੀ ਨੂੰ ਰਾਜਗੱਦੀ ਤੋਂ ਹਟਾ ਕੇ, ਪੰਜਾਬ ਦੇ ਰਾਜ ਦੀ ਗੱਦੀ ਹਥਿਆ ਲਈ

1841: After a struggle for power, Maharaja Ranjit Singh Ji's second son, the grandson of Sardarni Sada Kaur Ji (Kanhaiya Misl) and the son of Maharani Mehtab Kaur Ji (Kanhaiya Misl), Maharaja Sher Singh Ji is installed as the new Sovereign of Panjab.

# Shaheedi of Sardar Zorawar Singh Ji Kahluria

ਸਰਦਾਰ ਜ਼ੋਰਾਵਰ ਸਿੰਘ ਜੀ ਕਹਲੂਰੀਆ ਦੀ ਸ਼ਹੀਦੀ

1841: Sardar Zorawar Singh Ji Kahluria attains Shaheedi whilst battling to take control of Tibet.

# Kingship Of Maharaja Duleep Singh Ji

ਸਰਦਾਰ ਸ਼ੇਰ ਸਿੰਘ ਜੀ ਦੇ ਕਤਲ ਤੋਂ ਬਾਅਦ, ਸਰਦਾਰ ਦੁਲੀਪ ਸਿੰਘ ਜੀ ਨੂੰ ਪੰਜਾਬ ਦਾ ਨਵਾਂ ਮਾਹਾਰਾਜਾ ਨੀਅਤ ਕਰ ਦਿੱਤਾ ਗਿਆ ਅਤੇ ਮਾਹਾਂਰਾਣੀ ਜਿੰਦ ਕੌਰ ਜੀ ਨੂੰ ਮੁੱਖ ਮੰਤਰੀ ਬਣਾਇਆ ਗਿਆ

1843: After Maharaja Sher Singh Ji's assassination by the Sandhawalia Sardars, Maharaja Ranjit Singh Ji's youngest son, Maharaja Duleep Singh Ji, is installed as the new Sovereign of Panjab. Maharani Jind Kaur Ji acts as Chief Minister to handle the affairs of the state until Maharaja Duleep Singh Ji is deemed mature enough to handle the responsibility for the Kingdom of Panjab.

# Passing Of Kavi Santokh Singh Ji

ਅਕਾਲ ਚਲਾਣਾ ਕਵੀ ਸੰਤੋਖ ਸਿੰਘ ਜੀ

1843: Kavi Santokh Singh Ji passes away after producing the literary works of: Garab Ganjani Tika (1829), Valmiki Ramayana (1834), Gur Pratap Suraj Granth (1843).

# BIBLIOGRAPHY

PUBLICATIONS

Anand, Anita. Sophia - Princess, Suffragette, Revolutionary. Bloomsbury Publishing, 2015

C. Banerjee, A. The Khalsa Raj. Abhinav Publications, 2003

Darshi R. A. The Gallant Defender. B Chattar Singh Jiwan Singh, 1999

Davey Cunningham, Joseph. History of the Sikhs. Oxford University Press, 1849

K. Malhotra, Karamjit. The Eighteenth Century in Sikh History: Political Resurgence, Religious and Social Life, and Cultural Articulation. Oxford University Press, 2016

Kaur Sekhon, Harinder. Singh, Patwant. Garland Around My Neck, The Story of Puran Singh of Pingalwara. UBS Publishers Distributors, 2001

M. Juneja. M. Biography of Bhagat Singh. Modern Publishers, 2008

Mahmood Keppley, Cynthia . Fighting for Faith & Nation: Dialogues with Sikh Militants. University of Pennsylvania Press, 1996

Maharaja Duleep Singh. Maharaja Duleep Singh Centenary Trust Publications,1995

Prison Meetings of Bhagat Singh with Bhai Sahib Randhir Singh, Bhai Sahib Randhir Singh Trust Publications

Pettigrew G. Joyce. The Sikhs of the Punjab: Unheard Voices of State & Guerrilla Violence. Zed Books, 1995

S. Bains, K. Sikh Heritage in Paintings. Abhinav Publications, 1995

S. Mann, G. Singh, K. Sri Dasam Granth Sahib, Questions & Answers. Archimedes Press, 2011

S. Brar, K. Operation Blue Star: The True Story. UBS Publishers Distributors, 1993

Sekhon Singh, Dr. Awatar. Singh, Dr. Harjinder India Kills the Sikhs. Guru Nanak Institute of Sikh Studies and Sikh Educational Trust, 1993

Singh, Kushwant. A History of the Sikhs, Second Edition. Oxford University Press, 1999

Singh, Sangat. The Sikhs in History. Uncommon Books, 2001

Singh Madra, Amandeep. Singh, Paramjit. Warrior Saints, Four Centuries of Sikh Military History Vol.1. Kashi House, 2013

Singh, Patwant. M Rai, Jyoti. Empire of the Sikhs, The Life and Times of Maharaja Ranjit Singh. Peter Owen Publishers, 2008

Singh Wouhra, Trilok. His Imperial Majesty Maharaja Duleep Singh, King of Lahore, 2003

Singh Syan, Hardeep. Sikh Militancy in the Seventeenth Century: Religious Violence in Mughal and Early Modern India. I.B.Tauris, 2013

ਸਿੰਘ ਐਮ. ਏ, ਪ੍ਰੋ ਕਰਤਾਰ. ਸਿੱਖ ਇਤਿਹਾਸ

ਸਿੰਘ, ਸਵਰਨ. ਸਰਦਾਰ ਭਗਤ ਸਿੰਘ

ਸਿੰਘ, ਕੇਸਰ. ਸ਼ਹੀਦ ਉਧਮ ਸਿੰਘ

ਦਿਉਲ ਸਿੰਘ ਐਮ. ਏ, ਪੀ. ਐਚ. ਡੀ, ਡਾ ਗੁਰਦੇਵ. ਗ਼ਦਰ ਪਾਰਟੀ ਅਤੇ ਭਾਰਤ ਦਾ ਕੌਮੀ ਅੰਦੋਲਨ

MUSEUMS

Army and Empire, First World War, India's independence, Independence and Partition: 1947, Second World War, Sikh Collections. National Army Museum, London

Britain becomes a World Power, Expansion and Empire, The Indian Portrait 1560-1860, The Raj and the Indian sub-continent. National Portrait Museum, London

Continuing traditions in the Panjab 1849-1900, Maharaja Dalip Singh, Military Sikhs, Sikh objects from the V&A Collections, Sikhism & the City of Amritsar, Sikh historical photographs, The Panjab and the Rise of Sikh power, The Art of the Sikh Kingdoms, The Sikh wars & the annexation of the Panjab, The Court of Maharaja Ranjit Singh. Victoria & Albert Museum, London

Invasion of Punjab, Sikh Holocaust, Sikh Women, Sikh Timeline. National Sikh Heritage Centre & Holocaust Museum, Derby

Maharajah Duleep Singh (1838 – 1893). Norfolk Museums, Norwich

Sikh Collections. Brighton Museums, Brighton

GOVERNMENT

Allegations of UK involvement in the Indian operation at Sri Harmandir Sahib, Amritsar 1984. Ministry of Defence, United Kingdom

Komagata Maru Archives. Government of Canada, Canada

The Foreign Secretary's statement to Parliament on the Indian Operation at Sri Harmandir Sahib in 1984. Foreign & Commonwealth Office, United Kingdom